Princess Alannah's

GLOWING ADVENTURE

Written by **Sarah Bankuti**

Illustrated by **Jairalin Repalbor**

Princess Alannah's Glowing Adventure
ISBN Paperback: 978-1-7778428-7-1
ISBN Hardcover: 978-1-7778428-6-4
Text Copyright © 2023 by Sarah Bankuti
Illustration Copyright © 2024 by Jairalin Repalbor

Story written by Sarah Bankuti
Illustrated and Designed by Jairalin Repalbor

Edition 2024

Princess Alannah's
GLOWING ADVENTURE

This book belongs to:

_____

Princess Alannah, who lives in the Golden Reef, has NF - a condition that causes beauty marks to appear on her skin.

EMERALD
LAGOON

GOLDEN REEF

Every month she follows a little fish's emerald glow to see the healers.
Her tail is not as strong as other mermaids, and she needs her friend Scoot
to help her, but that doesn't stop her from having amazing adventures.

WAKE UP!

Alannah's mom urged her
daughter rushing into her room.

"YOU'RE GOING TO
BE LATE TO SEE THE
HEALERS - AGAIN."

Alannah yawned wishing she could go back to sleep.

"Remember," her mom said, "try to stay on the path. No wandering off this time" Alannah smiled sheepishly. She couldn't help it if everything she saw was just begging to be explored! But from the look on Mom's face, she was serious.

";Okay, Mom. I promise!"

I'M UP, I'M UP

Soon, Alannah and her friend Scoot were happily swimming along the emerald glow path on their way to see the healers.

"I THINK THIS IS THE RIGHT WAY THE PATH DOESN'T SEEM AS BRIGHT THIS MORNING THOUGH."

Scoot said, looking around.

MAYBE THE GLOW FISH IS STILL SLEEPING
I WISH I WERE STILL SLEEPING.

Alannah said and yawned.

Suddenly, Alannah noticed something in the distance.

"SCOOT, IS THAT A SHIPWRECK? I'VE NEVER SEEN THAT BEFORE."

"OH, NO! I THINK I BROUGHT US THE WRONG WAY!"

Scoot cried.

WELL, WE CAN'T HAVE WANDERED THAT FAR FROM THE PATH

Alannah said.

LET'S JUST LOOK FOR THE GLOW

Scoot nodded.

His eyes darted up and down the path. "Ah there!" He finally shouted.

"I see something glowing behind that rock. Come on."

Peeking over the rock, Alannah saw a group of electric eels dancing together, their electric glow lighting the water around them.

"Hi!" Alannah said. "We're trying to find our way back to the glow path. Have you seen the glow fish?"

"NO GLOW FISH, BUT THE SEAGRASS MEADOW IS GLOWING MORE THAN USUAL TODAY."

The eels replied, pointing the way.

"But the glow wasn't coming from a glow fish.
It was coming from a smash of Jellyfish!"

WOW JELLYFISH!

Said Alannah. Admiring their beautiful colors.
"Uh-huh. Pretty.", Scoot replied.
"But not the glow we are looking for. Come on!"

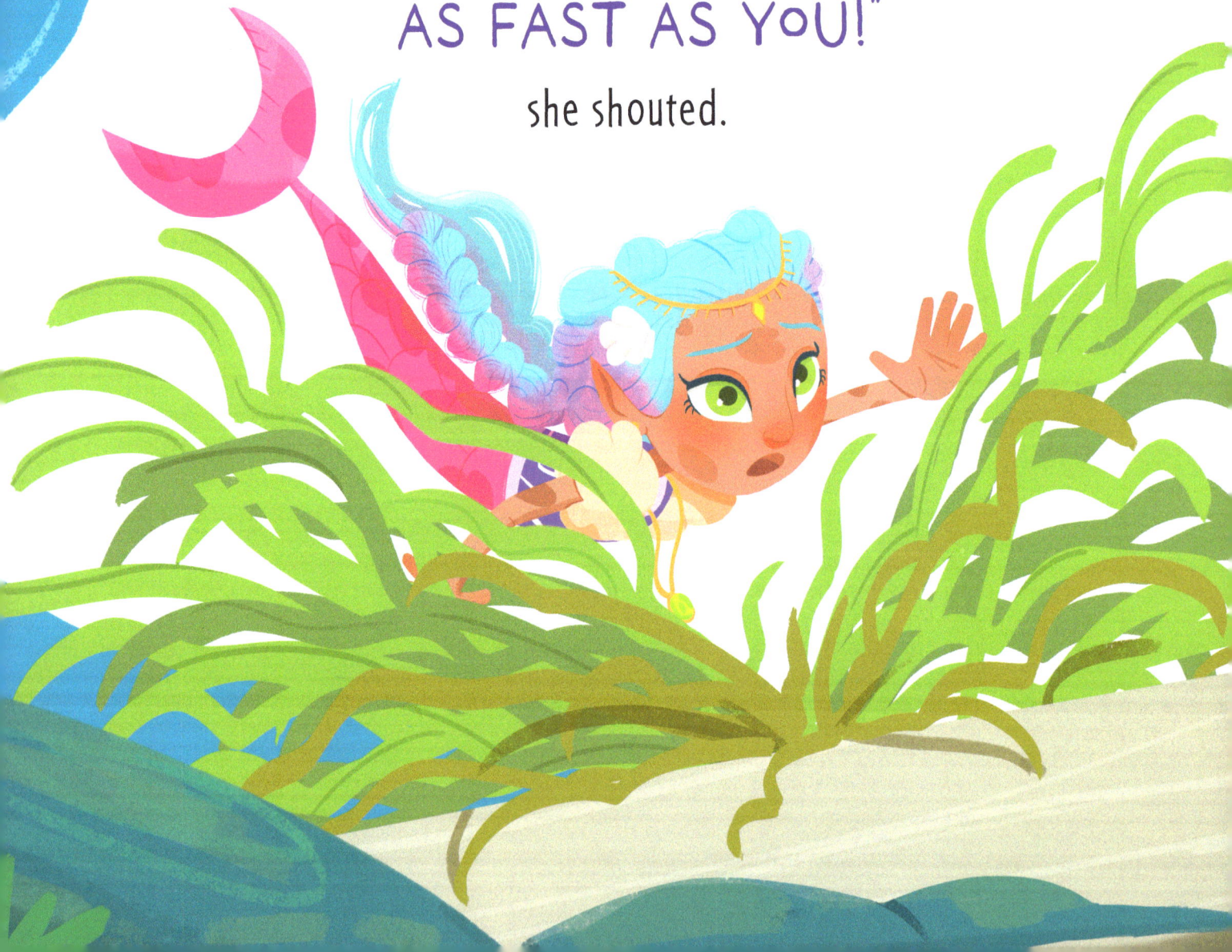

Scoot dashed forward through the sea grass, eager to find the real glow. Behind him, Alannah struggled to keep up.

"SCOOT! SLOW DOWN! YOU KNOW I CAN'T SWIM AS FAST AS YOU!"

she shouted.

Scoot immediately stopped and waited for Alannah.
"I'm sorry. I was so focused on finding our way back
to the path that I forgot you couldn't keep up!"
"That's okay," Alannah said. "Let's stay together from now on."

"LOOK!"
Scoot whispered,
pointing towards a cave.

""I DON'T KNOW ABOUT THIS, SCOOT,"
Alannah said, her voice trembling.

"Why would the glow fish be in a cave?" Scoot shook his head.
"It has to be somewhere! Now come on."

Keeping close to the sides, Alannah and Scoot edged past the glowing shadows on the cave walls. Suddenly, a loud shout shook the walls and rippled the water.

GO AWAY!

Alannah jumped in alarm.

"WE SHOULD
LISTEN
TO IT!"

She whispered.

But Scoot just kept swimming.

Taking a deep breath, Alannah followed . . .
And saw a small fish pressed against the cave wall.

"GO AHEAD, LAUGH AT ME
ALL YOU WANT, THEN LEAVE ME ALONE."

The fish said and began to cry.

"LAUGH?"

Alannah asked, swimming
towards the fish.

"BUT WHY
WOULD
WE LAUGH
AT YOU?"

"Because I am different from the other fish," sobbed the fish.
"None of them glow like I do - Why do I have to look different?"

Alannah sighed. She knew how it felt to wish with all your heart to be like everyone else. But she also knew that her differences were what made her special.

"EVERYONE IS BORN DIFFERENT AND THAT'S OKAY."

She said gently.

"BEING DIFFERENT MEANS, WE CAN LEARN FROM EACH OTHER."

"SOMETIMES WE NEED TO BE BRAVE TO EMBRACE OUR DIFFERENCES. IT IS WHAT MAKES US UNIQUE."

Said Scoot.

"I JUST GLOW, THERE'S NOTHING SPECIAL ABOUT THAT."

The fish said.

"Don't you know?" Alannah asked.

"Without you, merpeople wouldn't be able to find the enchanted forest and see the healers. Your glow lights the path and shows us the way."

MY GLOW DOES ALL THAT?

Wondered the glow fish.

BUT I'M JUST A LITTLE FISH.

IT'S NOT OUR SIZE THAT MATTERS,

Alannah said.

"EVEN THE SMALLEST OF US CAN HAVE THE **BIGGEST** IMPACT ON OTHERS."

"YOU MAY BE SMALL, BUT YOU LIGHT UP THE WHOLE LAGOON."

At Alannah's words, the fish glowed more brightly. He'd never dreamed that his glow was so important.

"Thank you!" He shouted and swam off, his glow lighting up the way to the enchanted forest.

"Look!" Scoot said. "I guess we weren't that far off, after all."
"Well, what are we waiting for?" Alannah said and smiled.

"ALANNAH, THERE YOU ARE!"

Called Ellie, one of her friends.

"Where were you?" "We were on an adventure!" Alannah said.
"A great adventure. I have to go and see the healers,
but after....I'll tell you all about it!"

The Real Princess Alannah

Alannah is a 7 year old girl living in Co Kerry Ireland with her mom, dad, little brother Adam, aunty Caitlin and her pet cat called Salem. At the age of 2 Alannah was diagnosed with a condition called neurofibromatosis type 1.

It causes inoperable tumours to grow on nerves. Alannah has one in her brain on her optic nerve and has spent many days in Hospital having brain surgeries, MRI'S and eye exams. She is also engaged with many medical services to monitor the tumours and NF1.

In 2022 she completed 70 weeks of chemotherapy to keep the tumour stable. The tumour has caused hydrocephalus and Alannah has needed 7 surgeries to date to alleviate the symptoms of this. Despite all these invasive procedures and medical days Alannah is a bright and bubbly little girl. She loves colouring, lego and telling jokes and always manages to smile even through her toughest days.

Thank you to the NF association of Ireland for all their help in creating a book series for children with neurofibromatosis. For more information please check out their **website:** www.nfaireland.ie

About the Illustrator

Jairalin Repalbor aka Bunbunillus lives in the Philippines and is a Freelance Illustrator who loves to work on Picture Books and Cartoon illustrations.

A passionate and skilled illustrator, she worked on several children's books, Mermaid's Don't Wear Floaties, B.e.e Smart and, much more. Jairalin's goal is to help the younger generation maintain interest in reading illustrated books. Through vibrant visual stimuli and good use of structure and color, Jairalin can help you achieve your goals and bring your ideas to life!

Instagram: @bunbunillus_art

www.ingramcontent.com/pod-product-compliance
Lightning Source LLC
Chambersburg PA
CBHW042114040426
42448CB00003B/276